From Candles to Chameleons
Memories of a Norfolk Man

Written by
Robert E Moore

Published by Strange Studios.

Text Copyright © 2021 Robert E Moore.

The right of Robert E Moore to be identified as author of this work has been asserted by him in accordance with the Copyright, Designs and Patents Act 1988.

Table of Contents

Foreword

As it says on the cover, this is a collection of my memories. Some may or may not be entirely accurate, but it's the best I can recall and it is all true.

Researching my family tree made me realise that without the knowledge of my late Mother and Brother to assist me, I knew very little about my predecessors.

I don't want this to happen to me. I want my children, grandchildren and their children to know about me and how I lived for the first twenty four years of my life.

Bawburgh

Bawburgh is a charming little village about five miles west of Norwich.

In summer my Wife and I often go there for a picnic by the river. We park the car and get out the folding chairs, sandwiches, a flask of coffee and something to read then settle down for a relaxing two hours or so.

There is a stone bridge to the left of us and a water mill to the right. Usually, there are young parents with babes in pushchairs and older children with nets trying to catch tiddlers in the river.

This is the England that I love and remember.

You may wonder about my fascination for this lovely village.

To explain this to you, I will have to go back to the very beginning.

Alburgh – The Beginning

We were born on 6th February 1939 at home in the village of Alburgh, South Norfolk, about three miles north of the small town of Harleston.

Philip came first and I followed minutes later.

Our mother, Rossie, must have been highly surprised to have given birth to twins. In those days, prior knowledge of the sex of your unborn child was unheard of and multiple births were rarely detected.

Granny Gooch (mum's mother) said that of course, *she* knew Rossie was having two babies because she could tell by the way mum was 'carrying'. Maybe she should have told the family doctor before he delivered us - he was clearly as surprised as mum and dad!

As twins we were not identical in any sense, me being small and skinny with brown hair and eyes whilst Philip was a chubby faced, blue eyed blond. I'm told I was active and outgoing whereas my twin was generally quieter and better behaved.

Father was christened Edward, but was always known as 'Ted' and sometimes 'Eddie'. A Hempnall man, he was the only son born to his parents, but had nine surviving sisters, so as children, we had a plentiful supply of aunts.

Dad worked alongside his father as a bricklayer's labourer and enjoyed the outdoor life. A keen gardener also, there was always plenty of fresh vegetables and fruit for his family. He wasn't a tactile man, we never had hugs or cuddles from him, to us he was just 'dad' and he always had our love and respect. Strict at times, he doled out punishment when deserved - often a 'clip round the ear' for me.

As well as mum and dad in the family was our sister Rita. She was born four years earlier in 1935. My younger brother Anthony came along in 1943, but more about him later.

One day when Philip and I were about two years old, mum was doing the usual Monday wash and had the old zinc foot bath full of boiling water on the kitchen floor ready to immerse the 'whites'.

We twins were walking by this time and to keep us out of the way, mum had left us to play in what we called the 'front room'. However, Philip wanted to be with her and toddled towards the kitchen doorway.

He tumbled down the steps between the two rooms, landing directly into the bath of steaming water. He was severely scalded and subsequently died.

In later years, I was to learn he had suffered from epileptic fits and it was believed that also contributed to his death. To her dying day, mother never spoke much about this event and it is my sister Rita who has always tended to Philip's little grave in Alburgh churchyard.

Rossie was devastated, Ted was away doing his bit for the war, and coping with two young children was too much for her. Having me around was a constant reminder of Philip. She turned to the family for help. Grandparents and aunts were duly consulted and the whole family thought it was best that I should be sent to stay with dad's sister Lily and her husband Fred's home in Bawburgh. They were childless and could give me the start in life I needed.
Another factor was that money was scarce and having one less mouth to feed would help Rossie out financially. Life was hard during the war years for the women left at home, always living with the threat that at any time a telegram might arrive informing them a loved one had been killed or missing on active service.

Growing Up at Bawburgh

I don't know how long it was after the death of my twin but I was duly taken to the house where aunt Lily and uncle Fred lived. Bawburgh is a small village about 5 miles west of Norwich and roughly twenty miles away from my mother and sister.

In the garden there were dozens of colourful polyanthus plants and I recall thinking how lovely they looked and even today, when I see these flowers, I think of the time I spent there with my aunt and uncle.

Whilst there my education started at the village school, although I don't have too many memories of this. One event that does stand out was when I won a picture. Lessons for the day were about finished and the teacher said that whoever raised their hand first could have the picture. I carried it home rather proudly!

Before I started school, about the time I began to talk, it was discovered that I was what was commonly called at the time, 'tongue-tied'. This is a 'restricted mobility of the tongue due to abnormal shortness of the tissue connecting the tongue to the floor of the mouth'. All this meant that I was unable to say words properly; for example, I would say 'gugar' instead of 'sugar'.

Aunt Lily took me to the Jenny Lind children's hospital in Norwich for a small operation to correct the problem. On arrival I was led into a huge room and seated on a chair. A nurse came in and gave me a child's book to look at, but I was too frightened to even open it. Some time later the nurse came back and took me into a different room where I was told to lay on the bed.
A mask was placed quickly over my face and I didn't remember any more. Aunt Lily told me later that the day after we returned home to Bawburgh the first words I spoke were, 'auntie, I can say sugar!'
One Christmas day morning, there were presents for me lined up on the settee. I wanted to know which was the one from my big sister. Aunt held up a book saying that it was the gift from Rita. I looked at that book many times.

Although I knew I had a mother, father and sister, to my knowledge I never saw them or had any contact and I had no memory whatsoever of my twin.

Maybe that was the reason I never questioned as to why I lived with my aunt and uncle.

Aunt Lily was very protective towards me and never allowed me out onto the road to play with other children. I believe she was fearful a vehicle would knock me down so I was restricted to the garden.

I spent a lot of time leaning over the garden gate, watching all the goings-on.

Every day I'd wait for uncle Fred to come home.

He worked at Thorpe railway station in Norwich, although in what capacity I have no idea. He'd let me stand on his bicycle pedal and then push me down the path to the back of the house. Once we were indoors, I'd sit on his knee and he would read to me the Rupert Bear strip from the newspaper.

One day when I went to sit on his lap he said 'Boy, I think it's about time you read this for yourself' and from then on I did.

We always had to say 'grace' before meals and these are the words my uncle used. Words I have never forgotten.

Thank God and thankee
What we've got is scanty
If there'd been more
We'd've had more
Thank God and thankee

Sometimes, aunt would make a batter (Yorkshire) pudding in a large shallow tin and we'd eat this with gravy before the main meal.

It all seemed perfectly normal to me.

I was told years later (by my Yorkshire born wife, Anita) that this was quite a common practice, the idea being that the pudding would fill you up so you didn't eat so much meat! Bear in mind that this was wartime still and everything was in short supply.

Rationing was introduced during 1940 because the German submarines were attacking the ships that were bringing food into our ports. Their objective being to starve the British making us weak and therefore more vulnerable. Hence, rationing was a way of making sure everyone had his or her fair share of the food available. Rationing meant that people were allocated a certain amount of food per week.

Every family member was issued with a book containing coupons that had to be exchanged for food.

Petrol and clothing were also rationed. Even for the people who could afford them, Many cars were left unused throughout this time.

A typical food ration for one person for one week was:
2oz each of butter, cheese, margarine and tea
4oz each of bacon and jam or other preserve
12oz meat, 2 pints of milk and just 1 egg.

Many people did like my uncle, growing their own vegetables and keeping chickens to supplement the meagre rations. Many times I'd help him to mix the hen food, potato peelings, tea leaves and bran.

One day we heard the siren warning of an air raid over Norwich.

All three of us dived under the table but I'm not sure what good that would have done if a bomb had dropped nearby.

Thankfully none ever did at Bawburgh, although Norwich wasn't to be so fortunate.

All rationing was finally abolished in 1954.

My aunt and uncle, as I've said before, didn't have children of their own, so it's very possible that they looked upon me as the son they never had.

I lived with them for about four years; in fact they actually wanted to adopt me.

I understand that mother was actually considering this but after a chat with her doctor who told her 'Bobby's place is with his mother', she told Lily and Fred, 'No, Bobby must come home'.

So it was, that one day, aunt Hilda, another of dad's sisters, who lived next door to mum and dad, arrived on Lily's doorstep and said 'I've come to take Bobby home'.

Aunt Lily packed my things and gave them to aunt Hilda along with one new laid egg.

'This is just for Bobby' she said.

Caring for me as always.

I was six years old and my time at Bawburgh was over.

Many years later when I had children of my own, I realised what it must have felt like for my aunt and uncle to have brought up a young child for four years and then having him being taken away.

It must have been exceedingly distressing for them.

As an adult I kept in touch with Lily and Fred until their deaths, Fred in 1965 aged 72, Lily in 1970 aged 76.

A headstone in Keswick Churchyard marks their final resting-place.

The Bawburgh house is still there; Now modernised, of course.

Whenever I drive by the house, I slow down and recollect on my happy time there.

Return to Alburgh

I don't remember the journey back to the home of my birth.

However, I do recall walking in through the front door and the first person I saw was a chubby little boy in a blue play suit standing behind a chair.

He was staring at me wide eyed and probably wondering who was this 'big' boy?

Whilst I'd been away, mother had had another baby, my little brother Anthony (Tony).

I wanted to see my sister, Rita, but she wasn't there, she must have been in school. I soon settled in as though I'd never been away.

The resilience of children!

Dad wasn't there either, being still attached to the army and stationed away. But the war had finished by this time and I often watched with my mother at the window, waiting and hoping to see him coming up the road.

When he finally did arrive, he brought presents and souvenirs from the war for us children and for mum he brought a leather shoulder bag, which he said was made by a German prisoner of war.

Earlier in the war, dad had lost his right eye.

In Normandy at the time, and held down by enemy fire, he happened to turn his head when a bullet (or shrapnel) caught his eye. He turned to the young soldier beside him and said 'Blast boy, I've been hit'.

The poor young man was too scared to help so dad crawled away and fortunately soon came upon a field ambulance. If he hadn't turned his head when he did, the wound would almost certainly have been fatal.

From that moment on, the fighting part of the war was over for dad. He was flown back to England and hospitalised. From there he went to Swansea in Wales to convalesce. Sometimes he would go for a walk around town and on his return there would be money or chocolates on his bed, left there by the Welsh people.

Being a soldier, often he would get into the cinema for free. I think this was common practice in a lot of cities and towns at the time, nonetheless, dad would never hear anything said against the Welsh people.

One of the stories dad used to tell was when he came across the dead body of a German soldier.

There was a ring on his finger that dad quite took a fancy to, but he couldn't get it off the swollen finger so he left it there. Some time later he walked past the body again and noticed that someone had cut off the finger and taken the ring. dad said that *he* would never have done a thing like that.

Whilst they were camped on manoeuvres, a deep trench was dug and a pole placed over the top.

This was their toilet!

Telling us about it dad joked that the trench was so deep that by the time you'd wiped your backside and buttoned up your trousers, your body waste had just about reached the trench bottom!

Once his recuperation was complete, dad was given leave to go home to see mum and his family.

All too soon he was back on duty, this time guarding German prisoners of war.

Because of his eye, often these men would spit at him and abuse him verbally.

Dad complained to his superiors claiming that he was afraid that he could easily be attacked from his blind side and was told in no uncertain terms that he wasn't the only soldier to have lost an eye.

A quick response from dad was, if that was the case, he couldn't be held responsible if any of his prisoners escaped!

That worked and for the remainder of his time in the Army he was based at Colchester, and put on light duties, mainly tending to the officers' gardens at his camp.

He would come home on leave regularly, which took a lot of the stress away from mum. At least she knew she wasn't going to receive the 'dreaded telegram'.

Dad would cycle the 50 miles home to Alburgh and when he returned to camp, mum cycled part of the way with him as far as Scole, about 11 miles away.

Scole is a village on the Norfolk/Suffolk border and on one of these journeys, dad asked mum if they were in Norfolk or Suffolk? A couple of men on bicycles were passing and one was heard to say 'I can't go any fudder' (further). 'Oh' said mum 'we must still be in Norfolk then!'

After the war, once settled back at home Eddie resumed his old job as a bricklayer's labourer. He provided well for his family although he was very careful with money. As kids we would laugh and say he would only light the lamp when you could barely see each other across the table.

We lived in a 'two up, two down' semi detached cottage in what is known as 'Vinegar Lane', virtually in the middle of a field - no flush toilet, electricity or other 'mod cons'.

To obtain water, there was a pump on the village main street with a huge wheel that had to be manually turned to raise the water.

Many years later, a tap was installed at the top of the lane, still a three-minute walk away but progress! There must have been gallons of water spilled in the lane over the years; as none of us children ever managed to get home with a full bucket.

Vinegar Lane ran off the main village road. There was a house at the top near the road, one half way down and our house was the last.

After school, I used to play with my pals and when tea was nearly ready, mother would go to the top of our garden, the nearest point to the road, and call my name.

'Bobby!' she'd yell. Dad said she had a voice like a sergeant major. Most times I heard her but on the occasions I didn't, she sent dad to find me and when he did, he made me run all the way home.

In the house adjoining ours lived one of dad's sisters, Hilda, and her husband Billy. He was the local postman, grave digger and also a bell ringer at the local church. Hilda was a character in the village and everyone knew her.
She would walk everywhere since she never mastered the art of how to ride a bicycle but it never stopped her doing her bit.

During remembrance week she could be seen walking around the village selling poppies. Us children would get one for a penny. she would visit the school and we would sit there with our penny clutched in our hand to be replaced with a poppy.

We were always in and out of each other's homes and most days she'd bring in her newspaper and read aloud to us.

Our favourite was 'The Boy John Letters.' Written in Norfolk dialect. These were the work of a countryman who wrote as he spoke and spelled as he pleased. It was never the same if anyone else read it out; it required aunt Hilda's broad Norfolk dialect to make it real for us.

They enjoyed having us children close by as they had never managed to produce any children of their own. Nevertheless, during the war, they took in an evacuee. It wasn't a great success for them in view of the fact that, according to mum, Hilda wasn't very motherly and the child spent most of his time in our home. Rita was about the same age and he must have preferred to be with her, his new friend. I never met him; he was long gone by the time I came back to Alburgh.

On the weeks leading up to Christmas, Billy would be busy delivering cards to the villagers and very often they would say to him, "Come on in Billy and have a drink!"

He never refused.

When he finished work, he would cycle down the lane rather unsteadily on his red postman's bike and when he reached his house he would simply fall off.

Hilda and Billy would often come in ours for a game of cards and Billy would frequently and loudly pass wind much to the annoyance of Hilda who called him a 'dirty bugger' but Billy didn't care. Us children laughed uproariously, we thought it great fun.

Tony and I shared a bedroom with mum and dad and I remember early one Christmas morning, dad kept shining his torch on the box at the bottom of my bed. I'd put it there the night before for father Christmas to put our presents into. By the light of the torch I saw something that got me even more excited. 'I've got a cowboy hat, I've got a cowboy hat', I shouted. Not only that, there was a toy gun with belt and holster too. I couldn't wait to show off my new toys to my chums. I felt like Roy Rogers (my cowboy film hero of the time).

I **was** 'Roy Rogers'.

Tony and I were getting older and it was decided we should no longer share our parents' bedroom.

The problem was where to go?

Next door Hilda and Billy had a spare bedroom but it would not be convenient for us and them to have to knock on their door every time we wanted to go to bed,   so, with their consent, dad cut a doorway through from Rita's bedroom into their spare room. This became our new bedroom!

As the house had no electricity, oil lamps and candles in candlesticks provided our lighting. Most of the candle holders were plain but some were ornamental and all usually had a spike or cup to hold the candle.

I recall going up the stairs to bed in the dark, feeling my way by touch, going down the two steps into Rita's bedroom, through the new door into our room and feeling for the chair by the side of the bed where I knew the candle and the matches to light it would be.
Mother never went out to work but she was always busy at home. Monday was washing day, Tuesday ironing and so on.

We didn't have a washing machine as such; it was a copper tub built into the corner of the kitchen. Before she could start the washing, a fire had to be lit under the copper. Sticks and old newspapers was the fuel used to get the water boiling. The water for the wash was collected from a pond in Billy's garden next door. There were rickety old steps leading down and an equally rickety handrail, not very safe at all.

After all the washing was done, to extract as much water as possible, it had to be put through a 'mangle'. This equipment consisted of two heavy rollers between which the clothes are passed. A side wheel to rotate the rollers turned a series of cogs. mum would turn the wheel and at the same time feed the wet laundry through the rollers. It actually worked rather well and items such as sheets, came out the other side pressed and needed no ironing.

The iron she used was a 'box iron'. despite being hollow inside it was actually quite heavy, The back had a sliding door to reveal the inside space.

She also had two iron shaped blocks and using tongs she would put them in the fire. When they were glowing red she would take one out using the tongs, then lift up the slide at the back of the iron and insert the red hot block and commence ironing.

When the iron cooled it was replaced by the other and the cooled one set back into the fire. She had to work with speed since the irons cooled quickly. The whole procedure was repeated many times on ironing day - what a performance!

Mother cooked in an oven that was set in the wall with a grate underneath, holding the fire to heat the oven. There was no thermostat, instead a device called a 'damper' was used. This was an adjustable plate set into the flue and pulled in or out to control the draught and thereby the temperature.

Quite a hit and miss affair I feel.

On the side of the fire were 'trivets', flat plates hinged to swivel over the flames. Pans of potatoes, vegetables, soups etc. were all cooked this way. When there were no meals being prepared, the kettle sat on the trivet, boiling away, always ready for that good cup of tea!

Bath night was every Friday.

The tin bath would be brought in from the shed and placed in front of the open fire. It was filled with water previously heated in the copper. One by one we all got into the same water.

I can still remember the smell of the carbolic soap and protesting loudly as mother scrubbed away at me.

Change came for us in 1954.

Dad later had the copper moved into the outside brick shed and decided to spend a bit of his hard earned cash and invest in a Calor Gas cooker and lighting.

This meant that we had a rather large cylinder of gas standing in the kitchen feeding mum's new stove and two lights, one in the kitchen, the other in the front room.

We still had to use candles in the bedrooms.

After putting up with the oil lamps, this was quite a luxury, also better for the eyes.

Even the box iron was changed for a gas model. A pipe attached to the wall lamp fed the gas to the iron. The naked flame was concealed in the body of the iron. A very dangerous method indeed.

In today's technical age, all this so far sounds awfully primitive, but it was how we lived at that time. We were happy and healthy, and that's all that really counts, whatever the decade.

Life in Alburgh

We had so much energy when we were young, unlike today in the age of computers, playstations, Ipods and the like.

We were always outside, climbing trees, wrestling each other or playing at being Cowboys and Indians.

When we got 'shot', we'd clutch our stomachs, make the appropriate noises and fall heavily to the ground.

We weren't hampered by health and safety regulations, we were so intent on enjoying ourselves.

But I have to say, Health and Safety is a wonderful thing. Many people have been saved from serious injury or death.

Tony was different, he wasn't as boisterous as me and when he was 'shot', he would fall down very gently.

He did however have talents I never had.

Quick minded and a very neat writer and in later years, he became a good cook, making celebration cakes for birthdays, weddings etc. Every year he baked an anniversary cake for the local radio station and became quite a well-known figure there, often being mentioned on their programmes.

I loved being out with my chums, and especially enjoyed flirting with the girls. Tony was always there, hanging around and this really annoyed me. I was afraid that if I did anything naughty or rude with the girls, he would tell mum or dad and I'd be punished.

I hit on an idea and persuaded Tony to do something wayward that would be met with disapproval. Once the deed was done, I said 'Right, if you tell mum and dad about me, I'll tell them about you'.

How devious can you get?

Poor Tony. It was emotional blackmail but I did love him just the same.

We would often go to the pictures at the nearby town of Harleston or Bungay. You could go in halfway through a film and when it ended, you could sit there and wait for it to start again and watch it up to the point where it was when you first went in, or see the whole programme again.

There were usually two films on in the programme, what we called the big picture and the little picture.

My favourites were the westerns. In one scene you would see the baddies getting away and then the hero would appear on his white horse and we'd all cheer like mad and he'd be going so fast. I used to think, at that speed, he could easily win the Grand National.

My cowboy hero at the time was Randolph Scott, he replaced   Roy Rogers. To me he was all man. I remember thinking what a wonderful uncle he would make.

We would leave our bikes in the shed adjacent to the cinema and the thought that they might not be there when you came out didn't even occur to us.

That's how it was back then. Today, you would need a heavy padlock and chain and even that's no guarantee that it wouldn't get stolen.

Our lane carried on further down past our house to a five-barred gate. Beyond that lay a large meadow, a stream running through it with a small stone bridge over.

In summer, buttercups, daisies and poppies grew in abundance. The stream was pure and clean to drink and you could safely eat your fill of the hedgerow blackberries without fear of them being contaminated by insecticides.

I'd climb the tree there - right to the top - and sit amongst the branches with no fear whatsoever. It was all so idyllic; most children nowadays couldn't possibly understand what it was like.

Today, the stream and bridge are gone, the meadow ploughed and the tree felled, never again to be enjoyed by anyone.

We had a wind-up gramophone in a cabinet. I used to love playing the old 78rpm records on it but sometimes the spring would wind down before the record had finished and the voices would get deeper and deeper so you then had to wind it up rather quickly to get it back up to speed.

One of my favourite records was one I kept playing over and over again. It was called the 'Maharajar of Magador'. My Father was so sick and tired of hearing it that he took the record, held it over his knee, and I remember thinking, "he's not really going to do it", but he did. He brought the record down on his knee and smashed it. I was devastated.

Looking back, if the situation was reversed, I would probably have done the same thing.

You can listen to it on YouTube but please be aware, I was young at the time.

As a boy, my favourite comic was the 'Beano', followed closely by the 'Dandy'.

I loved the characters, Lord Snooty, Dennis the Menace and Jimmy and his Magic Patch.

Jack Flash, another favourite of mine, came from a different planet and had wings on his ankles enabling him to fly. Aerodynamically this was impossible of course, but what kid cared about aerodynamics back then.

One day, dad went to clip the chickens' wing tips. This is normal practice, done to stop the chickens from flying over our fence but in my mind, I thought he was cutting off the whole wing. I wanted them to fit onto my ankles and fly like Jack Flash. What a disappointment.

Heating wasn't too much of a problem in the kitchen and front room, the fire was almost always lit, but upstairs was a different matter. In winter, if we were cold in bed, dad's army greatcoat was thrown over us.

When it was really cold there would be lovely frost patterns on the windowpanes. Extremely exquisite designs, no two being similar. Often they were so dense that even the strongest fingernail couldn't scratch them off but even if you did, it would freeze over again almost immediately.

On these cold days, getting out of bed was unpleasant. No warm carpet met your feet, just icy, cold lino. Tony used to take a glass of water to bed with him and in the morning, there would be a thin film of ice on it.

A rhyme we said was:

> 'Look out, look out Jack Frost's about,
> He will have your fingers and toes'

And often he very nearly did! We never lingered for long upstairs.
The toilet was another area we didn't hang about in for too long in winter.

No indoor flushing loo for us, oh no! A hut in the garden made from a combination of wood, brick and galvanised sheeting was our lavatory.

Inside, across the width of the hut, was a box with a hinged lid with a hole about the size of a dinner plate in the middle. Of course, if you were really posh, you would have two holes cut into the box, one for children and one for adults. A bucket inside the box acted as a toilet bowl.

When full, dad would lift the lid, take out the pail and bury the contents in a previously dug hole in the garden - dreadfully smelly! The trick was to never let the pail get too full.

Even the toilet paper we used was nothing like the soft tissue of today. On the back of the toilet door was a hook holding several squares of newspaper - this was our loo roll! I don't know if toilet rolls were in short supply or unavailable or whether it was another of dad's money saving ways. Whichever, the news print always rubbed off onto your backside.

Sometimes when mother lit the fire it would not get going.

She'd prop the poker up in front of the grate to 'draw the fire'. I don't know how this worked, but within minutes, the fire would be blazing away.

Well into her late eighties, mum still had a coal fire in the kitchen and often used the 'poker' method. I would tease her about this but she took it all in good part.

I was always on the lookout for new interests and whilst reading a magazine, I saw an advert for 'Ellisdons of Holborn' in London. They sold weird and wonderful things; magic tricks, jokes and novelties. I was hooked.

An apparatus called a 'Seebackroscope' - put up to your eye to see what was happening behind you; a vase - apparently empty, that would fill itself up with water; x-ray glasses - enabling the wearer to see through walls etc.

I rather fancied that one but for rather naughty reasons.

The one that appealed to me most was the 'Ventrilo' - 'learn to imitate bird sounds' the ad claimed, 'learn to throw your voice. Book on ventriloquism included'.

Without hesitation I sent for this miraculous device, believing I'd be able to do all these things and amaze my family and friends. Oh, the naivety of youth! All I succeeded in doing was to make unintelligible noises and dribble down my chin.

Not learning from my lesson, I sent for another device, this time a camera with a small hole where the lens should have been. Underneath was a stopper that pulled out revealing a tank to fill with water, in other words, I'm sure you can guess, a water camera. Anyway, armed with my new toy, I walked through the village and encountered a local lady by the name of Bessie Woolton.

'Can I take your picture Mrs Woolton' I asked innocently.
She posed for me but I said she would have to move in closer and she obliged. I pressed the back of the camera and a stream of water shot out and hit her full in the face.

'You little bugger!' she yelled but I was long gone.

I believe my son took after me regarding playing tricks on people.

I used to get up early in the morning for work and to avoid waking my wife I would put no lights on. Instead, I would walk along the hallway in the dark until I came to the bathroom door, open it softly and then slap the wall to my left feeling for the pull cord. It was slap slap click, slap slap click, every morning, only this time It was slap slap slap slap but no click. By this time the air was getting very slightly blue but eventually I found the pull cord... My son had taped it to the bathroom ceiling!

Whilst I was looking for a torch to find out what had happened, my son was laying in his bed silently laughing his head off.

As a family, we all went to 'Hemsby for a weeks holiday.

'Hemsby is a small seaside resort a few miles north of 'Great Yarmouth and is very popular with people with small families.

Whilst there my son had a throat infection so we saw the local doctor who prescibed an anti- biotic for him.

During the night he had a really bad coughing fit so my wife nudged me and said, "go and give him some of his medicine" so I stumbled into the kitchen all bleary-eyed, unscrewed the top off the medicine bottle and gave my son a spoonful.

It was only when I looked at the front of what I thought was the medicine bottle, I realized it was in fact, suntan lotion.

I made him drink lots of water and he came to no harm, and his infection cleared up.

Was it the suntan lotion?

When we arrived home we brought back a little present for one of our neighbors and she was very pleased with it, then my daughter piped up and said, "Yes, daddy won it on bingo!"

Kids. Can't take them anywhere.

Back to Childhood

I'd heard that my grandfather (dad's father) had a party trick that involved running a red-hot poker across the palm of his hand. I wanted to see this happen so the next time we went to grandfather's house, I hoped to see him perform this trick, although it wasn't really a trick at all. I noticed the poker in the fire was glowing red. Grandfather said to me 'smell my hand boy'. I did and it had a kind of tobacco aroma to it. He pulled the poker from the fire and ran it across his hand a couple of times. Holding out his hand to me once more he said 'Now smell it again'. This time it smelled of burnt flesh!

A tough man, my grandfather. It was said of him that if he wanted to put a line down a piece of wood, he'd not use a pencil or knife' he would simply use his fingernail!

One day, dad told me to go to the village garage to get a gallon of paraffin for the oil lamps.

Off I went on my bike with the empty can to do as I was told.

On my way back, I was cycling down the lane, one hand on the handlebar, the other holding the can of fuel, which, incidentally, had no cap on.

Quickly gathering speed, I was afraid to take my hand off the handlebar to apply the brake in case I fell off. The bike had a back-pedal brake, which meant that if I pedalled backwards, I would have stopped but I never thought to use it. So, I hurtled past the house shouting 'can't stop, can't stop, can't stop' and threw the can down. I ended up by the five bar gate, half the paraffin had gone and dad was *not* very happy.

We had relatives staying with us one Sunday for dinner. They all decided to go to the pub for a drink and mum left me with strict instructions to take the meat pie out from the oven once it was done. I know what you're thinking - but no, I didn't let it burn.
I duly lifted the perfect pie out of the oven and promptly dropped it on the floor where it broke into many pieces.
When they all arrived back from the pub, I met them at the door and said brightly, 'Does anyone like jigsaw puzzles?'

This time mum was *not* very happy.

My father was ill in bed one Christmas and mother sent for the Doctor. As he walked up the stairs to see dad, Doctor noticed one of our Christmas decorations in the shape of a cat with a long tail hanging on the wall. He leaned forward to touch the ornament and in doing so he stepped on the tail of our pet cat that he hadn't seen sleeping on the stair. The cat gave an almighty yowl and the Doctor said 'Oh, that's how it goes', thinking the ornament had made the noise.

Mum and Tony laughed about that for many years.

We had no television to watch so we listened to the radio, or wireless, as it was called then. It was powered by an accumulator (battery) which had every so often to be taken to the local garage to be recharged - this was my job.

We'd listen to 'Dick Barton, Special Agent'. When it was announced on the wireless it would be followed by this rousing piece of music called 'Devil's Gallup'. You can listen to it on YouTube.

We'd all sit around the wireless in rapt attention and listen to the exploits of Dick Barton and his two cohorts, Snowy and Jock.

'Journey into Space' was another programme I loved, along with a western called 'Riders of the Range' which featured a dog called 'Rustler'

I mention this because when our black spaniel 'Pippy' died, I was pretty upset. So, a few days after, dad brought home a puppy. He set it on the floor and it ran straight to me. I had my very own 'Rustler'.

More Stories of Alburgh

Every Wednesday at school, a taxi would arrive to take the boys to woodwork classes in the nearby town of Harleston.

Mother used to give me a shilling (5p) and a sixpence (2½p).

The shilling was for a fish and chip lunch, and the sixpence to spend as I wished. I was always torn between buying a cream cake or a comic. Sometimes the cake won sometimes the comic!

I was never terribly good at woodwork although I did manage to make Dad a pipe rack and Mum a clothes horse which she used for many years, so I couldn't have been that bad.

We had a little shop in the village. As you walked in the door you were faced with a counter with the shopkeeper behind it waiting to serve you. Either side of you were two little bench seats where you sat, waiting for your turn to be served.

It all seems so very quaint now.

Apart from the village shop, we had a rounds-man call with the main groceries.

You knew from one week to the next how much it was going to cost almost to the nearest penny.

Prices didn't fluctuate than as they do today. I liked it when the rounds-man had called because the box he delivered the groceries in became my ship, my car or whatever I wanted it to be.

Life was so simple.

As a family, we often cycled from Alburgh to Hempnall; about five miles away to visit mother's aunt Lena and her husband uncle Jack.
Both mum's and dad's parents lived in Hempnall as well as other relatives so it's not surprising that in later years we moved there.

Lena would say to uncle Jack, 'Come on Jack, give the children a copper or two'. He'd pick up a black bag, put in his hand and pull out a handful of coins. mother said that if there was any silver in his hand it would go back down the bag a lot faster than it came up. We usually received two or three coppers each, about one and a half pence today. It was always spent on sweets.

They only had one child; a boy called Reggie who was unfortunately killed in the far east during the war. I don't remember him but apparently he held me in his arms when I was a baby on one of the few times he came home on leave. How hard it must have been for them to lose their only son.

It was on one of these cycle rides to Hempnall that something happened that we laughed about for many years afterwards.

We were on the outskirts of Alburgh when we heard someone shouting.

To our left was a cottage where a lady called Alice Clack lived.

She was sitting on her outside toilet with the door wide open! 'Cooee' she yelled out, waving to us. She was completely oblivious to what she was doing or where she was, but that was Alice all over. A real character just like my aunt Hilda in that respect.

The first time I ever saw a dead body was when I was about 13 and it was that of my Great aunt Lena who died in 1953.

Her husband Jack had passed away about a year earlier so Lena was living with us. She went to Ipswich to see her brother Harry and his wife but on the way home, she was taken ill. A few days later, she died.

I came home from school and mum told me what had happened and asked if I should like to see her. I took one look and ran from the room crying 'Oh, how horrible'.

But it wasn't really; her face had lost all the wrinkles and she looked very peaceful. She laid in her coffin in our front room until the day of the funeral. It was a highly polished casket with real brass handles as Lena had said that was what she wanted.
For many years afterwards, in that room, I imagined I could smell the polish from her coffin.

When she was only five years old, mother's father died as the result of an accident. He worked on the land and was on a ladder fixing the cover over a haystack. The ladder slipped, he fell to the ground and subsequently died from his injuries.

In time, my granny met Arthur Gooch and they married. A lady from the village nicknamed him 'Tatty' - no one seems to know why - and that is what we always called him, never grandad.

They produced a son, Wilfred; a half brother for Rossie and uncle to me. Wilfred remained a bachelor and, at the time of writing, still lives in the house in which he was born.

Wilfred was a typical country yokel and in later years taught me a lesson in humility. I had just bought my first vehicle, a ford Anglia van for just £25, quite a bargain.

I took my van to show it off to Wilfred and said to him, how much do you think I paid for it.

Under my breath I was thinking, "you haven't got a clue."
He looked all around it and then said, £25.

It was then that I realized, he wasn't as naive as I first thought. He might have spoke like a yokel but he read the newspaper from cover to cover and probably knew more about world affairs than I did, despite having traveled around the world for almost seven years.

I learnt then, never judge a book by it's cover.

Granny Gooch suffered from a condition known as 'St Vitus Dance'. This is characterized by uncontrollable jerky movements of either the face, arms or legs. I believe hers was restricted to face and arm since she easily managed to pedal her cycle to Alburgh every so often to bring us some sweets.

It was thought she may have developed this complaint as a result of nearly drowning as a child.

I'm horrified now when I think of how, as a boy, I would laugh at the twitches and jerks over which she had no control. Children can be so cruel.

Mother and granny both smoked cigarettes, as most people did back then.

One particular day, they were in the local shop and granny was telling the shop keeper that she was suffering from a rather bad cold. He pulled out a packet of cigarettes and said 'I don't suppose you can smoke then?' mum said that granny's hand shot out quicker than a snake's tongue.
She may have had an affliction but she certainly wasn't stupid.

After Grannie Gooch and Tatty passed on, Wilfred continued living in the cottage which incidentally dated back to the early 1700s.

Anita and I met in 1991 and it was then that we used to go and see Wilfred on a regular basis, and also to take him out.

We took him to a supermarket once and his surprise at all the food on display was almost childlike. The only shop he knew was the local village store. Another time we took him to a garden centre and just before we went in he said, "do I have to take my hat off?"

He may have been naive but he certainly knew how to be polite.

He relied a lot on his next door neighbors, Sylvia and Andy.

They did his laundry, and because all he had was one cold water tap in the kitchen. He had to rely on a chemical toilet which Andy very kindly emptied into a hole in Wilfred's garden.

Unfortunately, Andy died suddenly and it was up to me to do this rather unpleasant job. I didn't mind this of course but I worried that if the weather was bad or through illness, I couldn't get there to do it.

Wilfred by this time was in his late seventies and diabetic. We thought maybe a care home was the answer, bearing in mind he had lived on his own for so long he was probably very set in his ways.

Tentatively we approached Wilfred with the idea and to our surprise he was all for it, and so it was arranged.

He settled in rather well and believe or not, one of the residents was his former school teacher and remembered him!

In the few days before Christmas we would take him his presents with strict instructions not to open them before the big day but it was a waste of time. Wilfred had no self restraint, and we knew for a fact that no sooner had we left the care home, he would open his gifts.

Wilfred was at the care home for about three years. On the 31st of July 2012, he died peacefully in his sleep. He was eighty two.

At school, one of our teachers was Mrs Parks who gave us, amongst other subjects, religious instruction.

This lesson ended with a hymn.

She'd play the piano, thumping the keys and singing 'Onward Christian

Soldiers' in her stentorian voice. It was one of our favourites and we'd sing it with gusto.

On one occasion during the hymn one of the boys decided to pass wind. When our laughter subsided, she demanded 'Would someone please open the window'. She was not best pleased.

One day at school we had a nature lesson and the subject was roses. The class discussed this for a while then the teacher asked if anyone could name another prickly plant. When she mentioned the word 'prickly' my ears were deaf to anything else she said because I knew the answer! My hand shot up and teacher said 'Yes Bob?'

'Porcupine, miss' I replied.

The rest of the class were highly amused by my answer.

I thought she was going to say 'prickly animal'.

If I had listened properly, I would not have been the butt of my classmates jokes for the next few days.
Perhaps this was an indication of what I was to be like in later life, always jumping in head-first without really listening to what was asked of me.

I loved November 5th - I'd go out at night with my pals, our pockets full of penny bangers; 'little demon', 'thunder flash' to name a couple and they really did bang, they were almost like mini hand grenades. As a dare We would light them and see how long we could hold them before they exploded. How stupid can you get. My pals and I were never hurt - we were lucky, many kids were seriously burned playing this silly prank.

I can remember when My sister had her first bicycle, well maybe not her first but certainly her first new one. she had saved up her money religiously every week and when it was delivered to her she handed over her money and took posession of it rather proudly.

In those days when you bought a bicycle, it usually included a basket at the front attached to the handlebars or a carrier at the back over the rear wheel. A little pouch at the back of the saddle containing tools, a bell and a pump, and a front light powered by a dynamo.

I mention this because I was in a discount store in Norwich with my Wife and I pointed to a shelf and said,"what are those?", she replied, "mudguards for a bicycle."

I couldn't believe it, and all of a sudden I had this wild case scenario whereas I would go into a cycle shop to buy a bike.

The salesman would show me a selection of frames and I would choose one.

He then said, "Now what about wheels?"
"Yes." I said, "I'd better take a couple of those and also a handlebar."

"I also recommend a saddle." he said, "otherwise it could get quite uncomfortable while you're riding your bike."

"Ok." I said, "And some pedals." And so it would go on.

I sincerely hope this is not a sign of things to come.

Sometimes on a summer Sunday, as a family, we'd cycle to a nearby place called 'Mendham' where there was a river.

Dad would hire a rowing boat and the five of us would clamber aboard. Me acting the clown as usual would rock the boat. Mum and Rita screamed at me to stop but I thought that was hilarious. In fact it was downright hazardous. None of us wore life jackets or could swim. I dread to think what would have happened if the boat had overturned. We never thought of the danger, to us it was just good fun.

An event happened one day that really upset me.

At the back of our house we had a square water tank that was about half full at the time. Early one morning we heard the cat meowing, we simply thought it was crying to come in the house. When we finally got up, we opened the door to let the cat in and it wasn't there. It had fallen in the water tank and drowned. Even today when I think about it I get upset.

Mr Leverett, a friend of dad's, once asked me if I wanted to earn some money.

Of course I said 'Yes, what do I have to do?'

'I've got a job hoeing the beet in this field' he said, 'I want you to follow me and pull out the ones I miss.'
This enabled him to work more quickly.

Imagine a large field with rows and rows of plant seedlings.

"Hoeing the beet" is taking out the bulk of the plants and leaving a sturdier one a certain distance apart.

I started well enough but the rows seemed to go on forever and I was becoming bored and tired. Mr Leverett could see this and said 'you'll be all right tonight when you've got a piece of paper to rub between your fingers'.

I thought 'my God, he's going to give me ten bob' - slang for ten shillings (50p). I started again with renewed vigour and sure enough, at the end of the day, he gave me a ten shilling note.

That Saturday, I took a girl to the cinema. We walked into the foyer, me waving the ten bob note in the air and said' Two one shilling (5p) seats please'. I felt like a king. Mind you, we had to sit on hard wooden forms. The more expensive seats were at the back priced at half a crown.(12 . 50p.)

In 1953 I went to Holt Hall for six weeks, as had my sister Rita three years earlier. At that time, children from small village schools were invited to attend.

Holt Hall is a boarding school about 50 miles north of Alburgh and run by the Education Committee.

The idea was to broaden the students' outlook and prepare them for life in the outside world. The school was set amongst woodlands and had two lakes. When these became frozen in winter, we'd play ice hockey.

Near to the end of our term, parents were invited to the Hall to watch a play we staged for them.
I took the part of a Roundhead officer (nasty piece of work) in the time of King Charles 1 in the play.

'When Did You Last See Your father?'

The action was centered on the questioning of a young boy whose father was a 'Loyalist' and therefore a supporter of the King. We (the Roundheads) were hunting down the Loyalists, so I was one of the 'bad guys'. I was told I was quite good at acting.
Initiative tests set for us were great fun. One was a mock up of someone having fallen down a rock face and we had to rescue them. The teachers

watched and gave points accordingly.

Surprisingly, some months later I was offered another stay at the Hall, but for twelve weeks. Only a few were asked to return if they had distinguished themselves in some way the first time. I jumped at the chance as I had enjoyed the first stay and it also meant making more new friends.

Much the same as my first visit, I played sports, acted in another play, and so on.

All too soon the twelve weeks were up. It was time to return to Alburgh school but not for long as I was 15 and about to leave school and enter the outside world and the challenges that lay ahead.

I consider my time at Holt Hall was well spent and maybe helped choose the path I was to take in the following years.

Thelveton

I wasn't a very good pupil at school. Attention was usually given by the teachers to boys or girls who showed promise, unfortunately, I wasn't one of them. I had no clear Idea of what I wanted to do when I left school. Most of us simply wanted any job just to bring some money in, we didn't care too much what we did. If I had any ambition at all, It was to be trained as a butler in a big country house. Why this was so, I'm not really sure, but there was a time when the working classes were meant to know their place and look up to their betters (the aristocracy). Although by this time, 1954, that kind of thinking had almost disappeared, but it still prevailed in some areas. Maybe I had some unconscious desire to serve my so-called betters.

Whatever the reason, my youth employment officer arranged an interview. I duly turned up, accompanied by my mother, at the home of Sir John Mann and Lady Mann at Thelvethall hall near Diss. We had cycled from Alburgh for this meeting. Sir John looked down at me - he was a large man dressed in his country attire, including plus-fours - and thundered 'Have you struck fifteen?' 'Yes Sir' I replied meekly, and so it was I began my working life at Thelveton Hall.

Thelveton Hall

The job wasn't 'live-in' and the journey from home to the Hall and back was about a twenty mile round trip. Too far to travel every day even for me, a proficient cyclist.

Lodgings were the answer to the problem. Monday to Friday, I stayed with a Mr & Mrs Baker who lived in Thelveton village about a quarter of a mile from the hall so it was Ideal. They had no children of their own so I think they liked having me around. the rent I paid them probably helped. I'd go home to mum an dad at the weekends. This worked quite well.

My job included picking up the milk from the local farm on my way into work and leaving it in the Hall kitchen. I plucked pheasants and other game, skinned rabbits, chopped wood, polished shoes and cleaned cars etc.

My immediate boss was Stanley Cattermole. He was the chauffeur-come-handyman and he taught me how to drive. Not many people can make the statement 'I learnt how to drive in a Rolls Royce!', but I did! Never out on the road of course, only around the estate roads. It would be some years in the future before I passed my driving test.

I felt so proud when Lady Mann came to the garages where the cars were kept and say to me, 'Robert, Sir John and I will need the Rolls at 11am'. I would reply 'Yes Milady'. (I didn't touch my forlock) After a quick dust and polish, I'd drive the Rolls around to the front entrance door. Driving that car was a wonderful experience.

The Rolls

Sir John had three cars and I had to make sure they were all kept in pristine condition. I think Mr Cattermole had hopes of me becoming a mechanic, he himself was highly qualified, but I had no interest whatsoever. I recall the words he'd say to me 'induction, compression, power and exhaust'. He may as well have been talking double-Dutch: I couldn't get it through my thick head then and still don't have much idea as to how engines work.

The protégé Mr Cattermole taught before me went on to become a car mechanic with his own very successful business.

Three gardeners were employed at the hall, one of whom used to make fun of me.

One day in the garden, I saw him from a distance. I cupped my hands to my mouth and shouted out. 'Oi, bighead!', suddenly this figure arose from behind this bush.

It was Sir John.

I beat a hasty retreat. It was like something out of a Norman Wisdom film.

After a while, my desire to serve the aristocracy began to diminish especially when I was told to clean their muddy boots when they returned from a day out in the fields and woods shooting pheasants.

Talking with the gamekeeper one day, he asked why I came to work there.

I explained about wanting to be a butler initially but wasn't happy as I seemed to be spending the entire time outdoors instead of inside the Hall.

He said' Why don't you join the merchant navy and become a steward?'

Well, I'd heard of the Royal Navy, Army and Air force, but not the Merchant - I didn't even know what it was!

He talked a little more about it to me and I thought it wasn't a bad idea so I wrote to my employment officer for more details.

I received a load of bumph including a narrative on how running away to sea (which I wasn't about to do) could be a disillusioning experience. From that moment on, it was the start of another phase in my life. It was 1956 and I was seventeen years old.

I applied to join and was accepted for training on a ship called the 'Vindicatrix' based at Sharpness in Gloucestershire.

I had to have a clean bill of health, so a visit to the doctor and dentist was necessary. Doctor was OK, I had no health problems but the dentist was something else!

'Joles' was his name, an appropriate one for a dentist, like 'jowls'.

I'll certainly never forget it.

He gave me an injection to numb my gums and sent me back into the waiting room saying he would call me.

Well, I waited and waited and by the time he did call, the numbness had worn off. When he pulled the tooth out, I have never experienced such pain in my life!

That is why I'll never forget his name.
I don't know what my parents thought of me joining the Merchant Navy and although dad never said as much. I had the feeling that he would have liked me to enlist in the army - purely because he had served.

Mum was concerned about me going away of course, but she took the attitude that if I was happy, then that was all that mattered.

There were people who felt I'd joined the Merchant Navy to avoid being called up for national service but this was completely and utterly untrue. At that age I wasn't that devious.

I left with my parent's blessings.

Vindicatrix

My departure to London was from Diss railway station. Sir John Mann was traveling on the same train. He told me that if I waited for him on the platform at Liverpool Street, he would point me in the right direction for the underground tube station. He did this and from then on I was on my own.

I have always said that as you've got a tongue in your head, you can't go wrong and I never did.

Eventually, I found myself on another train, this time heading for Sharpness in Gloucestershire and the training school.

On the journey I got talking with other boys who were also heading for the school. We were all very apprehensive, having no idea as to what lay in store for us.

From Sharpness station, we all walked together to the camp.

As we entered through the gate, there were some boys standing off to the right. They were shouting things like, 'Just two more weeks, new boy' or 'You ain't never going home new boy'. I remember thinking 'what the hell had I let myself in for'?

Later, I heard that one or two of the boys had run away, but for me that wasn't an option - I'd made my choice and was determined to stick it out.

The quarters at camp were barrack type huts and it was one of these I was to share along with a dozen or so other new boys.

After we'd stashed our gear, we were taken a short walk to where the training ship 'Vindicatrix' was berthed.

As we walked on board, I noticed the galley (kitchen) was ahead of me. Inside, a large heavy set man was stirring something in a pot. He had a cigarette dangling from his mouth and was coughing profusely - talk about hygiene!

We were handed a plate that had a portion of 'sea pie' on it (honest) and then through another doorway to where two boys stood. One had a stack of buttered bread, the other had plain bread, slices of each were slapped onto our plates.

Walking through into the mess room, there was a series of long tables with bench seats. On the floor at the end of the tables was a canister containing tea or cocoa (no sugar), depending on the time of day.

In the weeks that followed, we were always hungry and we sent home for food parcels.

Some boys received sugar in their parcels and it was funny watching them surreptitiously trying to put it into their hot drinks without anybody noticing. Sometimes a boy would say 'Anyone want my bread?' and before he'd barely got the words out, a hand would shoot out and take it.

It was the survival of the fittest.

Before we'd finished our meal, someone would sweep the floor and the dust would billow up. As the tea canisters had no covers on, I tried not to think of the dust going in.

On the bow of the Vindicatrix was a figurehead of a woman and the tradition was (not officially) that every new boy had to touch the right breast of the figure. I was more scared of not doing it and losing face so I did as I was told. I dread to think what would have happened if I'd slipped and fallen into the murky water below.

The drop must have been about 30 foot plus the fact I couldn't swim!

When mail came for us, the officer would read out the name on the envelope and then flick it towards the recipient with unerring accuracy. I don't think he ever missed.

Just before lights out, one evening, some of the boys grabbed hold of me. They used a tin of boot polish on me and blackened my 'privates'. One had his foot on my face holding me down and I've never forgotten his surname - it was Bell.

Once the boys had had their entertainment at my expense.

I said 'Now you've had your fun, will you do something for me?'

'What?' they asked.

I looked at Bell and said 'Get him' and they did. He cried like a baby! Minutes later, it was lights out and I had a heck of a job trying to scrub off the boot polish in the dark with cold water.

The school trained two groups, either deckhands or stewards.

I chose the stewards.

I was taught the art of waiting and laying of tables amongst other things and passed an exam earning me a 'star' which I sewed onto my uniform sleeve.

A job in the cook's mess earned me another star to add to my first. I worked hard to earn my two stars although what good they did me I've no idea

On time off we walked to nearby Berkeley to see a film at the cinema there. The locals must have seen us as young tearaways as we walked back it the camp loudly singing the song, 'We are the Vindi boys'...

Films were shown at the camp also. Not the same type as the cinema though. These were educational.

One I recall informed us of the problems of mixing with girls of 'easy virtue' and the dangers of contacting sexual diseases from them. It was all very graphic and enough to put me off women, almost.....

After the six weeks training was completed, I wasn't immediately offered a place on a ship so I had no option but to return to my family home.

Walking down Alburgh Main Street in my uniform I sensed all eyes were on me and I felt really great.

Vindicatrix

Merchant Navy Days

A week after my return home, I received a letter informing me there was a ship called the 'Rattray Head' that I was to join at the Albert Dock in London.

It was with a certain amount of trepidation and excitement that I traveled to London and eventually found myself at Albert Dock.

I saw all the big ships, but couldn't find the 'Rattray Head'. As I walked alongside these giant monoliths in despair, a kindly dockworker pointed me in the right direction.

Now, in my imagination, I had visions of a large passenger liner with two red funnels and me wearing a white jacket, serving drinks to passengers from a silver tray. Oh, how dreams are shattered!

When I found the 'Rattray Head' it was no big ship with red funnels. It was a rusty pile of junk, not much higher than the quay itself. It was taking cement up to Grangemouth in Scotland and to return with coal from Tyneside.

I certainly wouldn't be serving drinks from any kind of tray.

Being a 'new boy' (again), I was the butt of my fellow crew members' jokes and innuendos. I'd learnt that this comes with the territory and you just have to get used to it.

My cabin mate was a chap called Mitch. He was Scottish and he thought he was a tough little bugger - compared to me, he probably was.

I turned in that first night and awoke the next morning to the ship's movement.

With mounting excitement, I rushed to the porthole and looked out.
Sure enough we were at sea. Well actually, the Thames estuary, but what did that matter?

My life at sea had begun!

I started my duties, which included peeling potatoes, washing dishes and such like. I was feeling pretty good, so much so, that I thought I'd have a cigarette.

What was all the rubbish I'd heard about seasickness? I felt fine as I smoked away.

By now, we were heading out of the estuary and into open sea.

I began to regret the necessity for a smoke. In fact I was feeling decidedly queasy and had to rush over to the side rail.

Now, if you are going to vomit over the side of a ship, make sure you lean over the leeward side and not the windward, otherwise you'll end up with the contents of your stomach in your face!

I learnt by experience that day and didn't do it again.

One night, the sea was extremely rough and as I lie on my bunk I could feel the aft end of the ship coming completely out of the water, the propeller spinning in mid-air, then crashing down again.

So it went on all night.

I felt as If every bone in my body was shattered. I wallowed in my misery. Working for the aristocracy didn't seem too bad after all.

Another occasion, I was sent to the next deck where there was a vegetable locker and told to prepare some of the veg for lunch.

The ship was rolling quite badly and I remember thinking 'Oh mum, why did I join the merchant navy? I wish I hadn't'.

Fortunately this phase was soon over and I was to enjoy my choice of job for the next seven years.

The ship's cargo of cement was unloaded at Grangemouth.

On the way back, we passed under the Firth of Forth Bridge and docked at Sunderland to pick up a cargo of coal.

My cabin mate, Mitch, and I went ashore to a place called the 'Broadway Cafe' and got quite friendly with one of the waitresses, Sarah, although not as friendly as we would have liked. But, we were young and inexperienced; I wonder where she is now?

Arriving back in London, the coal was being unloaded as Mitch and I went to go ashore. The wind was in the wrong direction and we were covered in coal dust.
I stayed with the Rattray Head for a few more runs up north and on 23rd

December, we were all paid off and once again I headed for home.

I had survived on my first ship.

That first Christmas, I spent at home. I got drunk on the day and threw up in my bedroom, unfortunately for mum who I left to clean up the mess.

I was becoming a hardened seaman!

A fortnight later, I traveled back to London and reported to the Shipping Federation.

The gave me a note to take to the Royal Mail Line office who put me on one of their ships, the Highland Chieftain.

This was more like the ship I had envisaged, although instead of red funnels, they were yellow. However, I was still a long way from becoming a steward and I signed on as a galley / cabin boy.

Crew accommodation was down below decks and centred around a square.

Within the square was the entrance to the hold. The opening was covered with boards that were held in place by metal girders the width of the hold. Tall round bars faced you when you came out of your cabin.

These were to prevent anyone falling into the open hold.

Of course, it was never open whilst at sea, only in port or loading / unloading cargo.

Some of the boys played 'dare' and walked across the metal girders when the boards were off. A risky business indeed.

I only did it once...

17th January 1957 we set sail for South America, entering the North Atlantic, calling at Lisbon and the Canary Islands, then into the South Atlantic to our next port of call: Rio de Janeiro.

The entrance to the harbour is most awe-inspiring.
Towering mountains back it; The spectacular sugar loaf mountain being prominent. A colossal statue of Christ surmounts the Corvocado Peak. If

only I'd had a digital camera then, the pictures I could have taken...

I feel so privileged to have seen all this.

From there to Montevideo and finally entering the River Plate and onwards to Buenos Aires.

Contrary to what most people think, the River Plate is not blue as portrayed in the film 'Battle of the River Plate'. It is in fact a muddy brown.

Buenos Aires at this time was in a period of political unrest and there were always armed soldiers patrolling the streets.

Sometimes we would fish from the aft end of the ship for catfish but when we saw the size of the fish the locals were catching, we gave it up as a bad job. Made ours look like tiddlers.

One day a shipmate and I went ashore taking with us our ration of cigarettes, hoping to sell them to the locals. An armed soldier saw us and beckoned us over.

He confiscated our cigarettes (for himself no doubt) and motioned us to be on our way.

Well, you don't argue with a man holding a gun, do you?

One of my jobs as a lowly cabin boy was to go around the passenger accommodation just before meal times with a small xylophone type instrument and play a tune (which incidentally I got quite good at) to let the passengers know that dinner was ready, then it was back to the galley to wash all the dirty dishes.
Coming back to our ship after being ashore, we passed another vessel that was being loaded with bananas. One of the dockers turned to us and gave us a whole bunch of them, we hung them in cabin and ate them as they ripened. They lasted us for quite some time.

Another time, we were docked in a place called Rosario; A small town not far from Buenos Aires.

To get into the town we had to cross a bridge. On the way back, alas, the bridge was closed, however, there was a ferry available; a man in a rowing boat.
As we approached the boat, a soldier appeared and his gun came up. I

72

looked into that little black hole and felt my legs turn to jelly wondering what was going to happen next? It certainly wasn't the time to be a smart arse. Seconds that seemed like an hour passed and we were allowed to cross in the row boat.

I didn't look back.

Still in Rosario, a couple of shipmates said they knew a place called 'Tigre' where we could ride horses. They askled if I wanted to go with them.

I did, but said that I'd never ridden a horse.

They advised me not to worry, just to tell whoever asks that I had.

Off we went on a train.

People were hanging on the sides for dear life - as they seem to do in Latin American countries.

At the stables, a man asked me If I had ridden before and I lied 'Yes."

I think he knew l was lying because he gave me the most gentle and oldest horse they had, probably the one they kept for children and the mentally unstable!

I managed to mount the animal and off we went, but I was no John Wayne and unable to get any speed out of it.

After messing around for a while, it was decided to call it a day and head back.

Do you know, that crafty horse sensed we were on the way home because he went like the clappers and I was hanging on for dear life.

I had never ridden a horse before and will never do so again.

I did one more trip on the Highland Chieftain and had what must be the quickest medical on record:
Doc - 'Were you here last trip?'
Me - 'Yes'
Doc - 'Were you all right?'
Me - 'Yes'
Doc - 'Next please!'
I was due a spell back at home and for a boy who had only ever been to

London once as a child, to have seen and done what I had in the last few months was quite amazing.

I took great pleasure telling friends and relatives all about my experiences.

I won't be mentioning all the ships I served on, some of these were home trade, meaning British ports, occasionally the continent, and there really isn't much I can say about them.

They were short trips and mostly uneventful.

Every trip I went on I always felt sea-sick or queasy for the first day. After that, the ship could roll or pitch or do whatever and it never affected me.

I could never understand this.

It was in later years that I found out that fishermen never liked to stay shoreside too long otherwise they lost their sea-legs.

That is what happened to me.

Whilst I had been away, things at home had been changing.

In 1957, Grandad Moore died.

Granny Moore continued to live alone in their house in Hempnall for a short while but then in '58 chose to go and live with Nellie, one of her daughters.

Father didn't want to see his parent's home go to another family and decided he would live there.

Another contributing factor to this decision was that my sister, Rita, was courting a chap named Bill.

They wanted to marry but had nowhere to live. So it was, that as mum, dad and Tony moved to Hempnall, Rita and her new husband took over our old cottage in Vinegar Lane, Alburgh.

I was still at sea and wasn't there for either the wedding or the move.

Granny Moore only lived a short while longer and passed away in 1959.

Many years later, Rita and Bill finally had electricity installed at their Alburgh cottage in Vinegar lane.
The first thing Rita bought was an electric kettle.

The last modernisation the cottage received under their ownership was in the mid 1990's, when a bathroom and flush toilet were fitted.

Rita and Billy lived happily together in the cottage until Bill died there in 2004.

Still with the Royal Mail Line, I joined the 'Potaro', sailing this time to Central America to the Maracaibo Lakes in Venezuela.

It was so hot there and the ship had metal decks.

I swear you could have fried eggs on them.

On leaving the Potaro, I joined the 'Darro'.

This was significant for me as it was on this ship I received my rating.

No longer a lowly galley / cabin boy, I was now a steward, earning the princely sum of thirty pounds ten shillings(50p) per month.

My mates said that as I was now in the money, I should buy some new gear.

As we were heading for South America again, I had to wait until we returned and docked in London. Once there, I bought myself my first pair of tapered trousers, a long, light blue jacket, red shirt and pink socks. To complete the 'look' I got a silver 'slim Jim' tie.

I thought I looked terrific but my mother called me a 'teddy boy'.

A lot of people said teddy boys were troublemakers, and some may well have been, but most were just young boys dressing in the style of the day.

On most of the ships I sailed on, I would take my record player with me and my records. On one particular ship (I can't remember which one) the Captain and the Officers were having a party and he sent one of the Officers down to my cabin, which I shared with three others.

He said to me, "The Captain send his compliments and would like to borrow your record player".

I said "Ok but it will cost him ten bob (50p)."

The Officer went away but came back a few moments and said, "The Captain says get stuffed."

He came back shortly afterwards with a ten bob note in his hand. (About five pounds in todays money).

I was pretty cheeky in those days.

I couldn't seem to get away from the Royal Mail Line. My next ship was the 'Loch Garth' which took me across the North Atlantic again.

We sailed within sight of the Azores, calling at Bermuda and Jamaica, then through the Panama Canal and along the west coast of America to San Diego, Los Angeles, San Francisco and on to Seattle and Vancouver.

The whole trip took fourteen weeks.

Sailing under the Golden Gate Bridge in San Francisco was an experience in itself.

You see the pictures of it but to be that close is truly astounding.

If you are in the vicinity of the mast as you pass underneath, you really get the impression it will hit the bridge. There's always some bright spark that shouts 'Look out, they've forgotten to lower the mast!'

Once docked, some of us would walk along Fisherman's Wharf, a famous tourist spot, and look across the bay to see the island prison of Alcatraz which held the gangster Al Capone and Robert Stroud, who was known as 'The Bird man of Alcatraz'.

I have an uncanny memory for remembering where I saw a particular film and the one I saw in San Francisco was called 'The House on Haunted Hill'.

It was considered so frightening that your ticket was your Insurance policy for a thousand dollars if you died from fright.

At least that's what it said on the front of the cinema...

I don't know if a claim was ever made but I saw the film years later on TV , and it was no more scary than Mary Poppins.

When I was in Vancouver, I went to Stanley Park and walked amongst giant redwood trees. I saw Indian canoes and totem poles and fed the red squirrels. A mate and I even took a row boat out on the lake!

Some of the ports we docked at were only for overnight and the stay not long enough to take a good look around the cities and towns.

It was a real shame because there was so much to see.

There's no easy way to describe the Panama Canal. It's so incredible. It was one of the most difficult and largest projects ever undertaken.

A Quick history:

The first attempt to construct the canal was under French leadership in 1880 but later abandoned.

The United States took over the project and the canal completed in the early 1900's.

By the time the 48 miles of canal was finally opened in 1914, a total of 27,500 workmen are estimated to have died in the French and American efforts. Malaria, Yellow Fever and landslides were the prime causes.

To sail through the canal is a humbling experience when you know the history.

Back on board ship, whilst in port, we sometimes had lifeboat practice.

The lifeboat, with us in it, was lowered into the water.

We were each given a ten foot long oar and had to row around the harbour.

It was chaos!

No one knew what to do, including the officer in charge. I'm just glad we never had to do this in a rough sea; We certainly would not have survived.

Following this shambles, we made it back to the ship. We then had to climb from the lifeboat to the deck via a rope ladder - no easy feat if you've never done it!

From this I learnt that if ever I was on deck in a rough sea and the ship was rolling, I'd drop to my haunches.

I had a real fear of running towards the rail and toppling over the side.

If you went overboard in a rolling sea, there wasn't much chance of survival.

Union Castle Line was my next shipping company and I was on the 'Kenilworth Castle' heading for Cape Town, Port Elizabeth and Durban.

We arrived at Cape Town during the night and I was totally unprepared for what confronted me the next morning when I went on deck.

The sight of Table Mountain was truly magnificent!

When ashore, there was an out of bounds area; District 6.

It was supposed to be extremely dangerous and best avoided.

We did take a rickshaw ride however. That was a different experience.
I don't think I appreciated the places I traveled to. I didn't realise how fortunate I was.

As we departed from South Africa, we found a stowaway on board.

It was a chameleon.

A wonderful little creature.

We'd put it on our clothing and watch it change colour to blend with the background.

It fascinated me the way it's eyes swiveled independently of each other.

Unfortunately after a few days it died, but we did give it a decent sea burial.

Back in England again I took a few weeks leave, then journeyed back to London where I 'worked by' on a couple of ships.

What this means is working on the ships whilst they were in dock, maybe for repair.

I then did a home trade run taking in Sweden, Germany and Holland.

In July 1959 I offered my services to the 'Port Line'.

They supplied me with a travel warrant and I made my way to Hepburn, a shipbuilding town near to Newcastle.

I was to join the ship 'Port Townsville' which was double-berthed alongside a recently launched ship, the Royston Grange which was waiting to be fitted out.
To get to the Port Townsville, I had to walk across the deck of the new ship, and vice versa if you wanted to go ashore.

I mention this because, many years later, in 1972, long after I'd left the Merchant Navy, the Royston Grange was en route from Buenos Aires to London carrying a cargo of chilled and frozen beef and butter.

It was involved in a collision with the 'Tien Chee', carrying 20,000 tons of crude oil, near to the entrance of the River Plate (South America).

The Tien Chee immediately burst into flames and the series of explosions that followed carried the flames to the Royston Grange.

Because of the butter cargo she carried, the flames quickly took over.

The ship didn't sink but all on board, sixty-one crew and twelve passengers, died.

Eight of the forty crew of the Tien Chee also perished.

Back to my travels and on15[th] July 1959.

The Port Townsville left Hepburn headed for Australia via the Panama Canal.

Perth, Adelaide, Melbourne and Sydney and Hobart in Tasmania were all port stops on this trip.

New Zealand also was on the itinerary with stops at Wellington, Napier and Auckland and back home via the Suez Canal.

This was my second longest trip, taking just over twenty weeks and was also the only ship where I had a cabin to myself.

The Captain of the Port Townsville... Now, he was something else!

'Moate' was his name and I swear he was slightly mad. He had a maniacal laugh and did inspections every day – the norm for cargo ships being two or maybe three a week.

A story doing the rounds at the time was that in the dining room during an inspection he saw a matchstick on the floor.

'Pick that match up before someone trips over it' he is reported to have said.

I can well believe it too.

On one occasion, whilst in port, it was the 'Tiger's afternoon off.

A 'Tiger' is the Captain's personal steward. I'm not sure where the name came from but there is a story that back in the days of old sailing ships, that the Captain had a bodyguard who wore a striped jersey – hence the name Tiger.

Before Captain Moate's Tiger left for his afternoon off, he put a fresh cloth, cutlery and laundered napkin on the captain's table ready for me to serve him at dinner that evening.

The Captain came in, sat down, opened his napkin and said to me, 'Steward, look at this'. I looked and saw the napkin was shredded at one end.

'Sorry sir' I said, not that I had anything to be sorry about, it wasn't my fault.

'And so you ought to be' retorted the Captain.

I muttered a few expletives under my breath as I took away the offending item and replaced it with a new one.

That night, back in my cabin, I was still smarting from the Captain's tirade and trying to figure out a way to get back at him.

A shipmate and I came up with an idea.

We obtained a clean napkin and tore it to shreds,leaving a small square in the middle. In this square I wrote:

Seasonable greetings Captain Moate
From a steward who unfortunately sailed on your boat
Remembering the night you were as bold as brass
I return you this so you can wipe your ass!

When I arrived back at home, I put the cloth into a shirt box, wrapped it and addressed it to Captain Moate c/o Port Line Shipping Co, London. The village postmistress kindly blurred the post mark so there was no way of telling from where the parcel had been sent.

I have no way of knowing if he received the napkin or not, but if he did, I would have given anything to see the look on his face.

'Of all the incidents that occur on board his ship, there's no way he'll remember this one', I thought...

Is there?

Having a cabin to yourself – albeit a small one – was quite a luxury.

I was to be on this ship for a reasonable time so I decided to make mine more homely by putting up curtains to the porthole.

I bought a length of material from a shop in Hepburn and the lady who served me offered to make it up for me. She was probably charmed by my devastatingly good looks and couldn't help herself...

My homely cabin was used as the venue for meetings and suchlike. I did card tricks and conjuring. I even put a notice outside my cabin door stating **'The Wizard's Den'.**

A joke I had pinned to my bulkhead was:

Old lady to mountain climber – 'Don't you feel giddy when you're
hanging from a rope hundreds of feet above the ground?'
Mountain climber – 'No ma'am, just highly strung!'

I often wondered what Captain Moate thought when he came round on inspections.

One place we called at in Australia (can't remember where) the dockers were on strike and we were asked if we would help with the loading of the cargo. Of course we said "yes."

Looking back, I'm not altogether sure whether we had a choice or not.

Anyway, we found ourselves on the deck of the hold while a crane lowered the cargo down to us to be unloaded.

When we had finished, the crane took the empty pallet back up but on the way it became detached from the ropes holding it.

Someone shouted 'Look out below!' and my shipmate, without even thinking, dived to the right.

A second later it hit the deck with such a force it seemed as if the whole ship shuddered.

If it had been me, I'm sure I would have looked up as the pallet was falling and it would have been curtains for yours truly.

One of my shipmates was a chap called Harry.

He was an unsavoury looking character. In fact he looked downright evil due to a long scar running down the side of his cheek.

I actually got on quite well with him. Being of slim build myself, I felt it prudent to keep on the right side of anyone who looked as though he could handle himself or of anyone who was bigger built than me.

Now, this Harry had sailed on a previous trip with a man called 'Pluke' who had borrowed money from Harry and had never repaid the loan.

Harry wasn't about to forget this.

He said to me, 'If you ever run into Pluke on your travels, just say to him 'Harry is looking for you".

I believe he said this to crew members on all the ships he sailed on.

Can you imagine the scenario? Every ship this poor bloke Pluke joins, there could be someone saying to him, "Harry is looking for you."
If it was me, I'd end up being a total wreck.

I arrived home in December 1959 in time for Christmas.

My sister Rita and her husband Bill came over to dinner and we stuffed ourselves silly.

After the meal, we'd play an assortment of games; Bingo, dominoes and a card game called 'stop the bus' – a game we still play with the family on occasion. Sometimes we played brag, but I wasn't too keen since my brother Tony invariably won.

All too soon the festive season was over and I had to report back to the shipping company.

When you sign on to a ship, it's not only for the duration of the voyage. It is in fact a two year article which means that the line could keep you out of the country for two years. However, if you reached at a British port during the two years, you could request to be signed off.

I was assigned this time to the 'Port Huon' and we sailed on 14th January 1960.

A couple of weeks out, we were informed we were on a MANZ run.

This is Montreal, Australia and New Zealand.

A long run.

The ship was an old rust bucket and I believe it may have been one of the last journeys it was to make.

At night, a few of us would go into the galley to make a sandwich.

We'd switch on the light and there would be cockroaches on the worktops and floor and they would scatter in all directions. We got used to it after a while.

Washing the dishes, there was nothing like 'fairy liquid' in those days. We used soft soap. A piece of this soap was cut into slices and placed in a tin that had holes pierced into it. A length of string was tied around the tin and hung over the hot tap. Once the water was running, voilà! We had soapy water!

The tables in the dining room had 'fiddles' attached to them. A kind of guard rail. They were mounted on hinges so that in the event of rough weather, they were raised to stop plates and cutlery etc from sliding off.

It didn't stop the things from sliding about the table though so we had to soak the tablecloth with water and that usually did the trick.

Soup was a bit of a nuisance too.

As the ship rolled the bowl had to be held accordingly to avoid a lap full of hot cock-a-leekie.

Dining room chairs had a chain connected from under the seat to a corresponding hole directly beneath. Again a rough weather measure – if the ship rolled, you wouldn't go flying.

If there was an officer that the stewards disliked, it had happened that the chain under his chair was unscrewed from the floor, leaving just enough holding it to appear normal...

This was a bit naughty though – I never did it!

Bear in mind, ships didn't have stablisers like they do on cruise ships today.

When engineer officers came into the dining saloon for breakfast, one engineer had to stay behind on watch.

Once the main group had finished, one went back on duty to relieve the one who'd stayed behind.

Now if this officer was a good old boy, he'd pop his head round the galley door and ask for a plate of egg and bacon to be left in his cabin and he'd eat it there.

This suited us fine. It meant we could clear up, have our own breakfasts and get on with our other duties.

One particular engineer however, insisted that he shower and change into his uniform before coming into the dining saloon for breakfast.

He was perfectly entitled to do this of course but it didn't endear us to him.

He would go through the complete menu and one morning, he wanted fish.

I called through the serving hatch "One fish please!'

My mate in the galley said 'Damn, I've just dumped it. Hang on a minute.'

He rummaged around in the waste bin until he found a complete fish. He washed it under the hot tap, slapped it onto a plate which I took and served to the officer.

He went on to order eggs and bacon followed by a griddle cake (a small pancake) and syrup.
By this time I was becoming really p****d off, as was my galley mate.

He took a griddle cake, threw it across the galley where it hit the bulkhead and slid onto the floor. Then he trod on it with a non too clean shoe.

Yet again I served the officer...

The moral of this little tale is, don't p**s off a waiter, he's the last person who has his hands on your plate.

Our first stop on the MANZ run was Curacao, an island in the Dutch West Indies. From where we were docked, we could see what we were told was Captain Morgan's Castle and we swam in the bay there.

At the Panama canal we stopped at the far end in a place called 'Cristobal'.

It was my 21st birthday and all my cards and good wishes from home were waiting there for me.

The timing was perfect.

The radio officer gave me a crate of beer which was a pleasant surprise.

When ships arrived at the canal entrance, they were unable to proceed through straight away.

There was a large 'holding' lake where the ships anchored until there were enough vessels to go through in convoy. From the lake, we could see the tops of the trees where the ground had been flooded to make way for the canal.

If you are a new boy, you're advised to hold on to all the bread you have so you can feed the mules that pull the ships through the locks.

This is a big joke.

The 'mules' are actually little trains!

About two weeks after leaving the Panama Canal, I contracted glandular fever and was confined to my bunk.

A female doctor who was working her passage (common practice) attended to me.

She had a moustache (honest) and she gave me a shot of penicillin in my backside. She didn't half pack a wallop.

I felt as though a donkey had kicked me.

I think she was a lesbian and had a deep rooted hatred of men.

My charm certainly didn't work on her.

It's hard to explain to people who have never been to sea what it is actually like.

You wake in the morning and it's sea, sea and more sea! Sometimes another ship would pass close by and we'd rush to the side and wave like mad.

We'd see whales spouting water, flying fish, - one even landed on our deck, and of course there were always the dolphins to be seen. Occasionally there would be the odd deserted island.

If you tell someone back home that you were in a rough sea, they'll smile and nod their heads, but they can never understand what it feels like.

Not only would the ship roll from side to side, but the bow would rise out of the water as well. This is called 'corkscrewing'. Now that my seasickness was under control I rather enjoyed the experience.

We were now heading for Australia and New Zealand again. What can I say about these places and the things we got up to without boring the pants off you?

Briefly, we went sightseeing, to the cinema a lot and, of course, hung about where the girls were.

One place that stays in my memory is the small town of Opua in The Bay of Islands in New Zealand.
There wasn't much for young men like us to do there at that time so my friend and I decided to find a bit of excitement.

We heard that there was a good place at Russell, a town across the bay.

How to get there?

Luckily for us, a couple of American tourists were going there on the car ferry and offered to take us. They had a crate of beer in the back and told us to help ourselves. Of course, we did.

We finally arrived at the hotel in Russell where the Americans were staying and they suggested we went into the bar whilst they booked in and then join us later.

Well, we had a gin, and another.

Our new friends eventually joined us and we drank another gin.

So it went on all evening.

I felt terrific but when I got up from my stool to visit the toilet, I just collapsed in a heap! The evening was over for me.

Someone very kindly took us back to our ship and I vaguely recall the journey. Despite this, I had kind of affection for Opua and Russell.

In 2007, Anita and I had the good fortune to travel to New Zealand.

Part of the holiday we stayed in Auckland with Anita's cousin Don and his partner Jan who made us very welcome and were only too happy to show us their lovely country.

One of the trips Don took us on included The Bay of Islands and included Opua and Russell. The hotel where I got very drunk nearly 50 years before was still there and we stopped off for a drink (not gin!).

It was all quite emotional for me.

Back at sea, the Port Huon was headed back across the South Pacific, to the Panama Canal and on to Vera Cruz in Mexico where regrettably we never had chance to go ashore.

That evening we were so excited to be there, no-one could eat their dinner. We took our trays on to the quayside and gave the food to the poor people who were always hanging around the dock areas. They dipped their fingers into the food and ate slowly as if they were afraid it would go all too soon.
Next stop was New Jersey where I did get an afternoon off.

I jumped onto a bus that took me under the Hudson River and on to New York to the biggest bus station I had ever seen in my life. Exits everywhere. I chose one and came out into what I wouldn't call the better part of NY.

I started walking, turning left and suddenly I was on Fifth Avenue, the home of the Empire State Building.

I really wanted to see this and found my way to the entrance.

Once inside I remember thinking what a lot of doors there were.

There were no signs anywhere.

It wasn't as tourist orientated as it is today, but a man showed me where to go to get to the top. I seem to remember that we had to change lifts half way up and we went so fast, my ears popped.

As expected, the view was magnificent.

I walked around and saw pictures of the building in various stages of construction.

Piece of History coming up:
In July 1945 a US Army 5-25 bomber piloted by Lt Col William Smith crashed into the 79th floor of the building.

Eleven office workers were killed as were the three air crew.

There was a recording booth and I made a record of my voice saying where I was but it has long gone. (The record, not the voice.)

Miraculously I found the bus station and the correct bus to take me back

to New Jersey where I rejoined my ship.
All in all, a most memorable afternoon.

At sea once more, our destination was Montreal, Quebec, and Toronto via the St Lawrence Seaway.

After all these years, my memory has failed me here although I do recall seeing the 'Château Frontenac' in Quebec - a world famous hotel.

At the time of writing, I looked it up on the internet and believe me, you need serious money to stay there.

My grandaughter went to university in Halifax, Nova Scotia, and whilst there, sent my wife and I a post card with Chateau Frontenac in the background.

Little did I know then that when I saw that hotel, my granddaughter would see it also.

The next part of our run took us through the Panama Canal yet again and back to Australia and New Zealand where we more or less visited the same ports as before.

If we were in the ports on a Sunday, sometimes the Captain would open the ship for the public to view. Whole families would come on board and we took great delight in showing everyone around, especially the girls. It made us feel important.

At last, we were on the final run of the trip, heading again for the Panama Canal, the Caribbean and finally to New York where we were paid off and flown home to England.

I wasn't too keen on the flying bit because five days previously, two airliners collided over Staten Island (New York) and 134 people died.

It was with a certain amount of relief as we came in to land that I saw the red London buses and knew we'd made it safely.

When I arrived home on Christmas Eve, I'd been away for three weeks short of a year, it was the longest trip I ever did.

That Christmas of 1960 was wonderful, with me being the centre of attention, telling anyone who would listen where I'd been and what I'd done.

I exaggerated wildly of course. I was always the showman!

It was on one of my train journeys from London to Norwich that I engaged in conversation with another young lad who was also in the Merchant Navy and like me going home on leave.

It came out in our chat that we both lived in the same village of Hempnall. As I'd only lived there for a short while and been at sea for most of the time, I didn't know too many people. He turned out to be the brother of a girl who I later met and eventually married.

The girl in question was called Vivien. In the early days of our courtship I was on leave. We were in Great Yarmouth and I decided I needed a new wallet.

Now Yarmouth, in common with other sea-side resorts, was lovely in the fifties and sixties (or maybe I'm looking back through rose tinted spectacles.)

You had your kiss-me-quick hats, comic cards (which I absolutely adored).
I laughed so much that I think Vivien pretended she wasn't with me.

Some were quite rude but there were two ways of looking at them.

There was also a man down Regent Street with two little monkeys who you could have photographed with your children.

It was cute at the time but looking back it was quite cruel.

Anyway, I went into this souvenir shop, pulled out my wallet and said to the assistant, "I need a new wallet, this one has just about had it."

He looked at it and said, "You've been letting too much sea water get to it."

"What do you mean?" I said.

He replied, "Well you're a seaman aren't you?"

Now how did he know? It must have been the way I walked.

Another time I was visiting Vivien's parents and her Mother gave me a cup of tea which I rather stupidly put on the arm of the chair I was sitting on.

Of course clumsy me knocked it off but i had time to think, "Oh my god, it'll ruin her carpet, she'll kill me!"

I reacted quite quickly and caught the cup before it hit the floor and not a drop was spilled.

The following two trips were much shorter; Each of just over six weeks duration.

The shipping line was Canadian Pacific Shipping Company and the ship was the 'Beaverlake' bound for Montreal.

I served mostly on cargo ships, having long since given up the idea of a passenger liner with red funnels.

The main reason I preferred the cargo ships was the cabin arrangements.

The most sharing a cabin would be four, whereas on a liner, it could be as many as ten - not my cup of tea at all.

Not only that, cargo ship crews were like a large family: you knew everybody. Not much chance of that on a huge liner.

When a ship came into port and had been cleared by customs, the taxi drivers would then come on board and shout out,'Taxi anyone?'

We would then grab a driver, give him our discharge book with a half a crown inside; If there was four of us then that would be ten shillings. In today's money that's roughly ten pounds.

He would then proceed to the dock gates, give the dock police the four discharge books, he would take out the money and give the books back to the driver and we'd be on our way to our prospective stations.

If no money exchanged hands, the police could in effect order you out of the taxi, search all your belongings and therefore hold us up. We just wanted to get home.

Of course, you also had to tip the taxi driver for knowing which dock gate to go out of and which policeman's cheek could be turned.

1961 sees me with yet another shipping line – New Zealand Shipping Co – on the ship 'Ruahine'.

Yes, it's off to Australia and New Zealand again, but with a different itinerary.

Papeete in Tahiti were new places to me.

Papeete was the location used for the 1962 film 'Mutiny on the Bounty'.

In the days of sailing ships, the natives would come aboard and hang garlands of flowers around your neck. Alas, times change and all I got was one single flower from a young girl carrying a basket full of them!

I loved being on the Ruahine.

In later years when I was settled in married life, I named my house after it.

Many more years later I discovered that Ruahine was Maori for 'The Old Lady'.
Quite appropriate really when all ships are referred to as 'she'.

After two trips on the Ruahine, I rejoined the Canadian Pacific Line and worked by on the 'Beaverglen' in dock for a couple of weeks before signing on the 'Beaverfir' for a trip to Montreal.

Beaverfir was quite a small ship, barely three thousand tons, and where I experienced the worst weather conditions I'd ever encountered.
We had to batten down the portholes and weren't allowed on deck.

The deckhands had to wear lifelines.

The odd thing was, I was never frightened, probably due to the fact I was young and foolhardy and didn't appreciate the danger of the situation.

The Beaverfir Captain was a scruffy individual. One of those men who'd worked his way up from deck hand so had none of the social graces other Captains may have.

A story was told about him that as he was so scruffy, he was arrested in Montreal for vagrancy.

He even took his bicycle on board when he sailed so he could go cycling in

Montreal but then he upset one of the crew members who threw the bike over the side and into the sea.

Despite the Captain and the bad weather encountered in the North Atlantic, I did one more trip on the Beaverfir and arrived back home in mid November 1962.

As utility steward aboard the Ruahine

On deck of the Canadian Star

Coming to the End of my Travels

I had reason to question my own mortality when a close member of my family died in December 1962.

I was working by on a ship docked in London and had an arrangement with my girlfriend Vivien, whereby I would phone the number of the phone box in Hempnall at an agreed time and she would be there to answer it.

One day I called and she answered, saying 'Your brother Tony wants to talk to you'.

He told me aunt Hilda had died.

I was in a state of shock.

I loved all my aunts but Hilda was special. She had lived next door to us all those years at Alburgh.

I realised how tenuous life was; How death could take you at any time.

Before that, I thought I would live forever.

The day of her funeral was bitterly cold, as was that winter.

I think it was called 'the big freeze'.

Hilda had many floral tributes; A testament to her popularity in the village.

It was unclear as to what happened, but she was found at the bottom of Vinegar Lane in a deep ditch. She had drowned.

In life she suffered from epileptic fits and it was thought she had had an attack and later as she went to hang out the washing, confused, she walked down the lane instead of the garden that ran parallel.
Hilda smoked and a local farmer told her that if she "kept smoking those things" she'd be dead within the week. In fact he'd "be surprised if she lasted the night out"...

It was a few hours after this conversation that she died.

Back with the Port Line again, I was assigned to the 'Port Wellington' and worked by for a couple of weeks, then we sailed on 8th January 1963 bound for Australia and New Zealand – where else?

Vivien and I were engaged by this time and eagerly awaited our wedding.

She wrote and told me she had found a flat for us at Unthank Road in Norwich.

It was rather costly though at three guineas (£3.15p) a week but it was worth it for us to start our married life together.

So this was one trip I couldn't wait to finish and I counted the days until I finally signed off on 5th June.

During my leave, Vivien and I were married.

It was a beautiful day. The ceremony was held in the local church, and the reception was in the village hall.

Vivien had arranged all this whilst I'd been away at sea.

That afternoon, we left by train for our honeymoon in London.

Unfortunately, we arrived to find we'd left the address of the hotel we'd pre-booked back at home.
Not what some might say a good start.

The taxi driver took us to a hotel he knew and we booked in.

If my memory serves me correctly, we only stayed the one night. Next day we did a bit of sightseeing then caught the train for home.

We enjoyed married life for a couple of weeks and then it was time for me to go back to sea.

After an emotional farewell, I boarded the train to London and reported back to the Port Line Co.

They gave me a travel warrant to Glasgow where I joined the 'Port Fairy' – no puns please!

I was missing my new wife dreadfully.

A few days later as we sailed to Belfast.

I made the decision there and then to pack it all in.

I told my boss who said I wouldn't find life easy shore side, but I was determined.

I was signed off and I boarded the ferry for Liverpool. I made my way to London's Liverpool Street station where I caught a train bound for Norwich and home.

I was 24 years old.

I'd driven a vintage Rolls Royce, had a ride in a rickshaw, sailed under Sydney harbour bridge and been to the top of the Empire State Building and seen many other wonderful places.

I'd served on 18 ships over six years, eleven months and three days.
I'd been to countries and places that most people of my age had never even heard of.

I was newly married.

My life at sea was over and a new chapter about to begin.

Up to Date...

The first job I took shore-side was that of bus conductor in Norwich. I'd collect the fares and hand out tickets to the passengers.

After approx 18 months I changed occupation and went to work at the famous 'Chocolate Factory' in Norwich.

Vivien and I had a daughter, Melissa and a son, Jeffrey.

Over the next few years we moved house a number of times; twice to Hempnall and several houses in the Norwich area.

We worked long hours and quite possibly this took it's toll on our marriage.

After 24 years marriage, Vivien and I went our separate ways.

Anita and I met in the summer of 1991. Both of us were divorced.

I worked at the factory for 30 years and took early retirement when it was closed down in 1996.

At the end of that year, Anita and I were married.

1996 was also the year that my father passed away.

My brother Tony continued to live with and look after our mother in their house at Hempnall.

Ten years later in June 2006, Tony was diagnosed with lung cancer and sadly died three weeks later.

Rita's husband Bill had died a few years earlier so she moved in with mum to care for her, alas poor mother never became reconciled to the loss of her youngest son and she died peacefully in her chair at home three months later.

She was 91.

The Hempnall house was sold.

In 1901, 12 members of the Moore family had lived together in that small three bedroom house. For the first time in well over a hundred years, the house was not inhabited by my family.

Acknowledgments

With grateful thanks to my wife Anita whose idea it was to put my story to paper.

My sister Rita, uncle Wilfred, and good friend Cissy, they helped to fill in details of my earliest years.

And to myself, for keeping my seaman's discharge book safe all these years.

Without It, details of ships, dates and destinations may have been less accurate.

Young and Innocent...

Printed in Great Britain
by Amazon

82087134R00068